RESCUE RIDERS

HELICOPTERS TO THE RESCUE!

BY FRANCES NAGLE

Gareth Stevens
PUBLISHING

Please visit our website, www.garethstevens.com. For a free color catalog of all our high-quality books, call toll free 1-800-542-2595 or fax 1-877-542-2596.

Library of Congress Cataloging-in-Publication Data
Names: Nagle, Frances, 1959- author.
Title: Helicopters to the rescue! / Frances Nagle.
Description: New York : Gareth Stevens Publishing, [2023] | Series: Rescue riders | Includes index.
Identifiers: LCCN 2021047144 (print) | LCCN 2021047145 (ebook) | ISBN 9781538278567 (set) | ISBN 9781538278574 (library binding) | ISBN 9781538278550 (paperback) | ISBN 9781538278581 (ebook)
Subjects: LCSH: Helicopters in search and rescue operations–Juvenile literature.
Classification: LCC TL553.8 .N34 2023 (print) | LCC TL553.8 (ebook) | DDC 629.132/5252–dc23
LC record available at https://lccn.loc.gov/2021047144
LC ebook record available at https://lccn.loc.gov/2021047145

Published in 2023 by
Gareth Stevens Publishing
29 E. 21st Street
New York, NY 10010

Portions of this work were originally authored by B. J. Best and published as *Helicopters*. All new material this edition authored by Frances Nagle.

Designer: Leslie Taylor
Editor: Kristen Nelson

Photo credits: Cover Mikadun/Shutterstock.com; pp. 2-24 (background texture) Pixel Embargo/Shutterstock.com; p. 5 aragami12345s/Shutterstock.com; p. 7 Martin Maun/Shutterstock.com; p. 9 Joaquin Barbara/Shutterstock.com; p. 11 branislavpudar/Shutterstock.com; pp. 13 Rihardzz/Shutterstock.com; p. 15 Monkey Business Images/Shutterstock.com; p. 17 Monica Garza 73 /Shutterstock.com; p. 19 BlueBarronPhoto/Shutterstock.com; p. 21 ALPA PROD/Shutterstock.com.

Printed in the United States of America

CPSIA compliance information: Batch #CSGS23: For further information contact Gareth Stevens, New York, New York at 1-800-542-2595.

CONTENTS

Boldface words appear in the glossary.

Flying High

What's that in the sky? It's a **vehicle** with many spinning blades on top. It doesn't fly as high as an airplane, but it moves fast in the air. It's a helicopter! It could be on the way to an **emergency**.

COAST GUARD

Helicopters are amazing! They can fly forward like an airplane. They also can fly backward, up, down, and sideways. Helicopters can **hover** and spin too. They can fly very low. Sometimes, helicopters take off and land on top of buildings!

Rescue Vehicles

Helicopters are able to fly just about anywhere! Because of this, they are often used for **rescues**. Rescue helicopters can be part of many emergencies. Each has a crew aboard specially trained for different kinds of rescues!

camts
Life-Guard
12

Mountain Flight

A mountain climber has fallen! A rescue helicopter heads to the area. A rescuer puts on a **harness**. They climb out of the helicopter on a rope. The rescuer finds the climber. They go up the rope together. The helicopter flies away.

Rescue on the Water

A boat has sunk! A person is lost in the water. The rescue helicopter flies over the water. It is windy. There are waves. The rescuer comes down and saves the person in the water. They use a rope to go up into the helicopter together.

Air Ambulances

Helicopters are used as **ambulances**. These air ambulances are used to transport, or move, people who are very sick or hurt. They may be far from a hospital or in a place a ground ambulance can't reach. These helicopters have **medical** supplies and a trained crew.

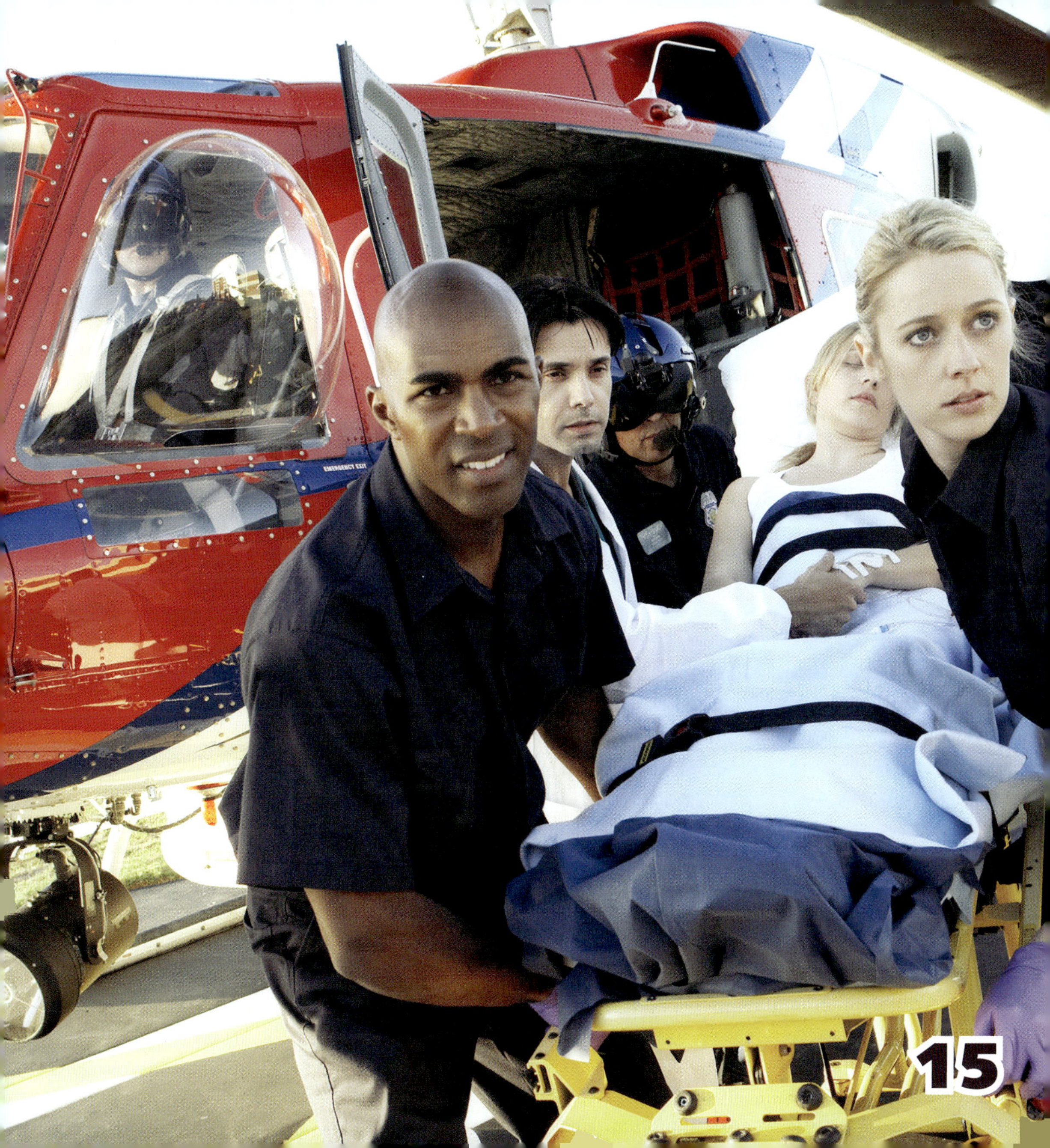
EMERGENCY EXIT

Disasters

Floods, earthquakes, and hurricanes are **natural disasters**. People may be stranded, or stuck, in their homes. Helicopters are used to rescue them. They are used to bring in needed supplies and people to help too.

Helicopters are sometimes part of police and fire departments. They help firefighters put out fires. Police use helicopters to look for missing people or someone who has done a crime. The **military** uses helicopters to carry soldiers and gear, and attack enemies.

Amazing Helicopters

Helicopters have so many uses! They can reach places other vehicles can't. This makes them **essential** to some kinds of emergencies. Crews train to fly helicopters on rescue missions. They save lives using helicopters!

GLOSSARY

ambulance: a vehicle used for taking sick or hurt people to the hospital

emergency: an unexpected situation that needs quick action

essential: extremely important

harness: something that holds a person

hover: to float in the air without moving around much

medical: having to do with care given by doctors

military: the armed forces

natural disaster: a sudden and terrible event in nature (such as a hurricane, tornado, or flood) that usually results in serious damage and many deaths

rescue: to free a person or thing from unsafe conditions

vehicle: an object used for carrying or transporting people or goods, such as a car, truck, or airplane

FOR MORE INFORMATION

BOOKS

Carr, Aaron. *Helicopters.* New York, NY: AV2, 2022.

Rossiter, Brienna. *Big Machines for Fire and Rescue.* Lake Elmo, MN: Focus Readers, 2021.

WEBSITES

Fun Helicopter Facts
www.sciencekids.co.nz/sciencefacts/vehicles/helicopters.html

Find out about helicopters and other vehicles on this website.

Paper Helicopter Video for Kids
easyscienceforkids.com/paper-helicopter-video-for-kids/

Read about helicopters and learn how to make one out of paper.

INDEX